Introduction

Are you familiar with Tina Cox? She is one of the most talented parchment artists you could wish to meet. She has inspired and motivated many thousands of crafters to take up parchment as a passion - myself included.

The artwork contained within this little book is a blend of Tina's own work, coupled with super samples from our talented Clarity Design team.

If you would like to get creative with Tina's Floral Doodle Collection, then this little ii-book will prove invaluable for projects, layout ideas and colourways.

Enjoy!

With love,
Barbara

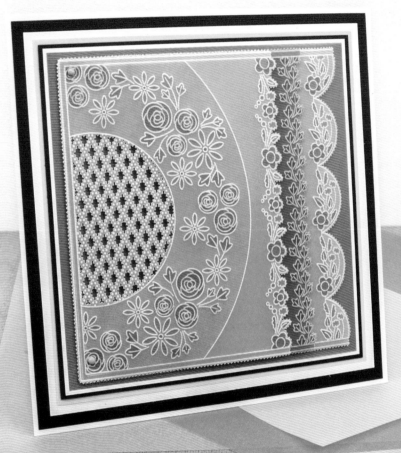

Lovely Layers
Tina Cox

Ingredients

TINA'S ROSIE DOODLE WREATH
GRO-FL-40831-03
TINA'S ROSIE DOODLE BORDER
GRO-FL-40832-09
TINA'S FLORAL DOODLE BORDER
GRO-FL-40833-09
NESTED SQUARES EXTENSION & ALPHABET FRAME
GRO-WO-40538-15
NESTED CIRCLES & FRILLY FRAMES
GRO-PA-40554-15
BASIC DIAGONAL PIERCING GRID
GRO-GG-40529-17

Tina has created a beautiful multi-layered design combining plain and coloured parchment.

How to...

1. Emboss the 8th & 9th squares from the outside of the Nested Squares extension plate on 2 sheets of clear parchment & 1 sheet of pink parchment paper.

2. Add the border designs as shown, each time using the previous border to assist in alignment.

3. Emboss the floral design and part of the nested circle onto the top layer of clear parchment.

4. Colour the floral designs on the reverse with Perga Colours Exclusive. Colour the background within the circle with Perga Liners blended with Dorso Oil.

5. Perforate, emboss and picot cut the grid design using the basic diagonal grid.

6. Perforate around all layers with the 2 needle bold perforating tool & picot cut.

7. Layer onto coloured backing paper using Pergamano Brads.

5

Best Wishes
Tina Cox

Ingredients

TINA'S FLORAL DOODLE WREATH
GRO-FL-40830-03
TINA'S ROSIE DOODLE BORDER
GRO-FL-40832-09
TINA'S FLORAL DOODLE BORDER
GRO-FL-40833-09
NESTED SQUARES EXTENSION & ALPHABET FRAME
GRO-WO-40538-15
STRAIGHT BASIC A4 GROOVI PIERCING GRID
GRO-GG-40528-17

Tina has perforated within the floral circle to give a lacy look.

How to...

1. On clear parchment paper, emboss the 8th & 9th squares from the outside of the Nested Squares Extension plate.
2. Emboss the borders and circular design including the greeting.
3. Using the grid, emboss dots around the border of the card and randomly within the greeting circle.
4. Colour the floral designs with Perga Colours Exclusive and behind the borders and circle with Perga Liners blended with Dorso Oil.
5. Perforate around the outer border and within the circle design using a 2 needle bold perforating tool and picot cut.
6. Mount onto coloured card using Pergamano Brads.

7

Hello
Tina Cox

Ingredients

TINA'S FLORAL DOODLE WREATH
GRO-FL-40830-03
TINA'S ROSIE DOODLE WREATH
GRO-FL-40831-03
TINA'S ROSIE DOODLE BORDER
GRO-FL-40832-09
TINA'S FLORAL DOODLE BORDER
GRO-FL-40833-09
NESTED SQUARES EXTENSION & ALPHABET FRAME
GRO-WO-40538-15
STRAIGHT SUPERFINE A4 GROOVI PIERCING GRID
GRO-GG-40626-17
NESTED OCTAGON EXTENSION & ART DECO ALPHABET
GRO-PA-40552-15

Tina has perforated and picot cut to create intricate corner designs.

How to...

1. Emboss the 3rd square from the outside on the Nested Squares Extension plate, the floral borders and circular designs.

2. Colour the floral designs on the reverse with Perga Colours Exclusive and behind the circular design using Perga Liners blended with Dorso Oil.

3. Emboss, perforate and picot cut the grid designs using the superfine grid.

4. Perforate around the outer border and around the designs with a 2 needle bold perforating tool and picot cut.

5. Mount onto designer paper or parchment using Pergamano brads.

9

Floral Picture Box
Tina Cox

Claritystamp

Ingredients

TINA'S FLORAL DOODLE WREATH
GRO-FL-40830-03
TINA'S ROSIE DOODLE WREATH
GRO-FL-40831-03
TINA'S ROSIE DOODLE BORDER
GRO-FL-40832-09
TINA'S FLORAL DOODLE BORDER
GRO-FL-40833-09
NESTED SQUARES EXTENSION & ALPHABET FRAME
GRO-WO-40538-15
STRAIGHT SUPERFINE A4 GROOVI PIERCING GRID
GRO-GG-40626-17

Tina has used the nested frame to create intricate layers on this stunning card.

How to...

1. Emboss the frame and circles on pink parchment and then repeat on clear parchment. Working on the pink parchment first, add the leaf design around the inner frame and in the circular panel.

2. Add whitework and colour on the reverse with Perga Liners, blending with Dorso Oil. Colour the frame with a black Perga Colour pen.

3. Using the Angle perforating tool, perforate, emboss and picot cut the inner part of the smaller circle.

4. Perforate the frame with the 2 needle tool and picot cut.

5. Emboss the remainder of the design on clear parchment, colouring as before.

6. Layer on to coloured card and attach with Pergamano brads.

A Daisy Chain for Tina

Josie Davidson

Ingredients

TINA'S ROSIE DOODLE WREATH
GRO-FL-40831-03
TINA'S ROSIE DOODLE BORDER
GRO-FL-40832-09
NESTED SQUARES EXTENSION & ALPHABET FRAME
GRO-WO-40538-15
STRAIGHT BASIC A4 GROOVI PIERCING GRID
GRO-GG-40528-17
DIAGONAL BASIC A4 GROOVI PIERCING GRID
GRO-GG-40529-17
NESTED OCTAGON EXTENSION & ART DECO ALPHABET
GRO-PA-40552-15

Josie has created a beautiful grid work border to show the Designer Backing Paper used in her design.

How to...

1. Emboss the 5th & 6th squares from the outside on the Nested Squares Extension plate and colour from behind using the Perga Colour Exclusive pens.

2. Emboss the floral designs and add whitework to the flowers and dots.

3. Add a greeting using the Nested Octagon Extension plate and then using the diagonal basic grid, perforate from the front to create a background pattern.

4. Using the border plate, create a ribbon/panel down one side and then infill with a pattern using the straight basic grid using a combination of embossing and perforating

5. Perforate around the outer border using a 2 needle bold tool and picot cut this and the grid design.

6. Attach to Brighton Rock Designer paper using Perga glue and embellish with gems, ribbon and Perga Glitter.

For You
Tina Cox

Claritystamp

Ingredients

TINA'S ROSIE DOODLE WREATH
GRO-FL-40831-03
TINA'S ROSIE DOODLE BORDER
GRO-FL-40832-09
NESTED SQUARES EXTENSION & ALPHABET FRAME
GRO-WO-40538-15
STRAIGHT BASIC A4 PIERCING GRID
GRO-GG-40528-17
NESTED CIRCLES & FRILLY FRAMES
GRO-PA-40554-15

Tina has used the colours of the Indian Summer Designer Parchment paper as the inspiration for her coloured work.

How to...

1. Using Indian Summer Designer Parchment paper, emboss the 2nd square from the outside of the Nested Squares Extension plate. From the Frilly circles plate, emboss the 4th & 6th circles from the outside.

2. Emboss the doodle designs and colour on the reverse with Perga Colours Exclusive.

3. Perforate around the border and inside the circles and semi circles with a 2 needle fine tool and picot cut.

4. On clear parchment, emboss the central design, the sentiment from the Plate Mate and the dots using the grid. Colour with Perga Colours Exclusive.

5. Attach to coloured card using Pergamano brads.

friEnds
ForeVer

Friends Forever
Glynis Whitehead

Ingredients

TINA'S FLORAL DOODLE WREATH
GRO-FL-40830-03
TINA'S FLORAL DOODLE BORDER
GRO-FL-40833-09
STRAIGHT PATTERN NO. 1 BORDER PIERCING GRID
GRO-GG-40350-14
NESTED SQUARES EXTENSION & ALPHABET FRAME
GRO-WO-40538-15
GRATITUDE & SENDING WORD CHAINS BORDER PLATE
GRO-WO-40564-09

Glynis has used the Border Piercing Grid to enhance her fabulous design.

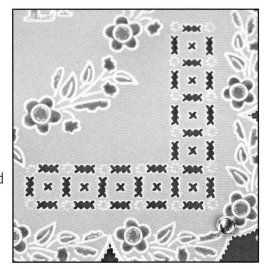

How to...

1. Emboss the outer circle of flowers and the sentiment.
2. Using the Nested Squares extension plate as a guide, emboss the scallops around the edge.
3. Working on the front, perforate the grid design.
4. Colour on the reverse of the floral designs with Perga Colours Exclusive.
5. Using the Pergamano 2mm star tool, emboss within the grid design.
6. Perforate around the design using a 2 needle bold tool and picot cut. Cut crosses and slots in the grid design.
7. Apply sticky ink and Perga glitter and mount onto coloured card using Pergamano brads.

Red & Silver Wreath
Chris Walker

Ingredients

TINA'S ROSIE DOODLE WREATH
GRO-FL-40831-03
TINA'S ROSIE DOODLE BORDER
GRO-FL-40832-09
NESTED SQUARES EXTENSION & ALPHABET
FRAME
GRO-WO-40538-15

Chris has added pretty gems to co-ordinate with the background on her lovely design.

How to...

1. On pink parchment paper, emboss the large circular floral design and circle. Emboss the inner circles and roses on a separate sheet.

2. Centre the wreath on the Nested Squares plate and emboss the 3rd & 6th squares from the outside edge.

3. Emboss the corner designs using the border plate.

4. Perforate around the outer border and the inner circle with a 2 needle tool and picot cut.

5. Shallow perforate around the inner circle piece using a semi-circle mini tool, re-perforate and picot cut.

6. Mount on to silver card using Perga Glue.

With Love

Tina Cox

Ingredients

TINA'S FLORAL DOODLE WREATH
GRO-FL-40830-03
TINA'S ROSIE DOODLE BORDER
GRO-FL-40832-09
TINA'S FLORAL DOODLE BORDER
GRO-FL-40833-09
NESTED SQUARES EXTENSION & ALPHABET FRAME
GRO-WO-40538-15
STRAIGHT BASIC A4 PIERCING GRID
GRO-GG-40528-17
NESTED OCTAGON EXTENSION & ART DECO ALPHABET
GRO-PA-40552-15

Tina has used Rainbow River Designer Paper to give her project a truly dramatic feel.

How to...

1. Emboss the 8th & 9th squares from the outside of the Nested Squares plate and add the floral design within it.

2. Using the grid, emboss dots within the double lines of the frame.

3. Add a sentiment using the alphabet from the Nested Octagon Extension plate.

4. Emboss whitework on the sentiment and dots and stipple the flowers.

5. Colour the floral detail from the reverse using Perga Colours exclusive. The borders are coloured with Perga Liners and Dorso Oil.

6. Add Perga Glitter using Sticky ink and a Mapping Pen.

7. Attach to backing paper with Pergamano brads.

Birthday Wishes
Amanda Williams

Ingredients

TINA'S ROSIE DOODLE WREATH
GRO-FL-40831-03
JAYNE'S BUTTERFLIES
GRO-AN-40319-03
ART DECO ALPHABET GROOVI BORDER PLATE MATE
GRO-MA-40348-13
NESTED CIRCLES & FRILLY FRAMES
GRO-PA-40554-15

Amanda has used Co-ordinating Shenandoah Designer Parchment & Paper for her eye-catching design.

How to...

1. On purple parchment paper, emboss the butterfly and paint with gold mica paint.

2. Perforate around the butterfly with a 2 needle tool and picot cut.

3. Emboss the 1st, 6th & 7th circles from the outside of the Nested Circles Extension plate on Designer parchment.

4. Add the floral design details and text using letters from the Alphabet Plate Mate.

5. Add whitework to the flowers and paint the letters with gold mica paint.

6. Colour on the reverse with Perga Colours Exclusive.

7. Mount onto Designer paper with Pergamano brads, aligning the parchment exactly with the design on the paper.

A Teal Rose Garland
Maggie Byford

Ingredients

TINA'S ROSIE DOODLE WREATH
GRO-FL-40831-03
TINA'S ROSIE DOODLE BORDER
GRO-FL-40832-09
NESTED SQUARES EXTENSION & ALPHABET FRAME
GRO-WO-40538-15
STRAIGHT BASIC A4 PIERCING GRID
GRO-GG-40528-17

Maggie has embossed dots within her 4 needle perforations to add extra detail on her elegant design.

How to...

1. Emboss the 3rd square from the outside of the Nested Squares Extension plate and centre the wreath within it.

2. Add a border design to the inside of the frame and then add whitework to the flowers and dots. Colour the flowers on the reverse with Perga Liners.

3. Add colour behind the wreath using Dorso Crayons and Dorso Oil.

4. Shallow perforate the outer border with a 4 needle bold tool. The grid to help with the alignment.

5. Emboss dots within the perforations using a 1mm embossing ball tool and then reperforate.

6. Picot cut the outer perforations and layer the design on to Shenandoah Designer Paper using Pergamano Brads.

Moody Pink
Karen Jackson

Ingredients

TINA'S ROSIE DOODLE WREATH
GRO-FL-40831-03
TINA'S ROSIE DOODLE BORDER
GRO-FL-40832-09
NESTED SQUARES EXTENSION & ALPHABET FRAME
GRO-WO-40538-15
DIAGONAL BASIC A4 GROOVI PIERCING GRID
GRO-GG-40529-17

Karen has added a grid design behind
the 3D element in her fabulous design.

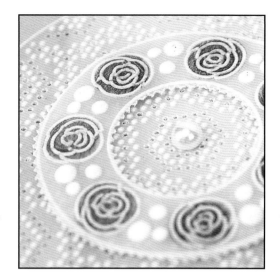

How to...

1. Emboss a frame using the 5th & 8th squares from the outside of the Nested
Squares Extension plate and the floral designs.
2. Add whitework to the flowers and dots. Colour from behind using Perga
Colour Exclusive pens.
3. Emboss and perforate the grid design in the central circle.
4. On a separate piece of parchment paper, emboss the smaller circle.
5. Perforate with a 2 needle tool around the main frame and the smaller circle
design and then picot cut.
6. Attach the design to Shenandoah Designer paper using Pergamano brads
and embellish with pearls.

Lacy Daisy Frame
Linda Page

Ingredients

TINA'S ROSIE DOODLE WREATH
GRO-FL-40831-03
TINA'S ROSIE DOODLE BORDER
GRO-FL-40832-09
NESTED SQUARES EXTENSION & ALPHABET FRAME
GRO-WO-40538-15

Linda has used the Pergamano Picot V perforating tool to enhance her pretty design.

How to...

1. On clear parchment paper, emboss the 7th & 4th frames from the outside of the Nested Squares plate. Emboss the border design and colour on the reverse with Perga Colours Exclusive.
2. Perforate the frame using a 2 needle perforating tool & picot cut.
3. Emboss the 7th & 3rd squares from the Nested Square Extension plate on Indian Summer Designer Parchment and the floral wreath designs. Colour on the reverse of the design with Perga Colours Exclusive.
4. Shallow perforate with the Picot V tool on the front and emboss within the perforations on the reverse. Re-perforate and picot cut from the front.
5. Mount on Designer Paper using Pergamano Brads.

29

Layered Doilies
Glynis Whitehead

Ingredients

TINA'S ROSIE DOODLE WREATH
GRO-FL-40831-03
TINA'S ROSIE DOODLE BORDER
GRO-FL-40832-09
TINA'S 3D FLOWERS & BUTTERFLIES
GRO-FL-40553-15
NESTED CIRCLES & FRILLY FRAMES
GRO-PA-40554-15
NESTED CIRCLES
GRO-PA-40051-03

Glynis has layered the circles on this gorgeous design to create a 3D design.

How to...

1. Emboss the wreath of flowers on the paler side of the Designer parchment (known as debossing).
2. Turn the project over and emboss the 6th & 7th circles from the Nested Circles plate. Then add the scalloped border.
3. On clear parchment, trace a circle with a pencil, using the 7th circle from the outside of the Nested Circles plate and use this circle as a guide to emboss the scalloped frame.
4. Emboss the small wreath on designer parchment paper.
5. Perforate all borders with a 2 needle tool and picot cut.
6. Create a 3d flower using the flowers & butterflies plate, using two flowers from clear parchment and one Designer parchment.
7. Attach to backing card, layering up and embellishing with a pearl.

If I had
a single flower
for every time
I think about you,
I could walk forever
in my garden.
C.Ghandi

If I Had A Flower
Dee Paramour

Ingredients

TINA'S ROSIE DOODLE WREATH
GRO-FL-40831-03
TINA'S ROSIE DOODLE BORDER
GRO-FL-40832-09
IF I HAD A FLOWER
GRO-WO-40604-04
NESTED SQUARES EXTENSION & ALPHABET FRAME
GRO-WO-40538-15

Dee has used one of our poetry plates as the focal point in her lovely card

How to...

1. Add a frame using the 4th, 8th & 9th squares from the outside of the Nested Squares Extension plate on the Indian Summer Designer Parchment.
2. Emboss the floral wreath and then the verse. Add a border within the frame.
3. Add whitework using embossing ball tools.
4. Colour the design with Perga Colours Exclusive on the reverse.
5. To create the intricate frame around the outside, use the semi-circle line from the border plate. Working round in one direction, and then flipping to infill and create a petal like design.
6. Perforate around the design and border using a 2 needle tool and picot cut.
7. Attach to coloured card using Pergamano Brads.

33

Claritystamp

Best Wishes Tag
Linda Page

Ingredients

TINA'S ROSIE DOODLE WREATH
RO-FL-40831-03
TINA'S ROSIE DOODLE BORDER
RO-FL-40832-09
NESTED SQUARES EXTENSION & ALPHABET FRAME
RO-WO-40538-15
NESTED TAGS
RO-PA-40654-04
OCTAGON EXTENSION & ART DECO ALPHABET
RO-PA-40552-15
STRAIGHT BASIC A4 GROOVI PIERCING GRID
RO-GG-40528-17

Linda has used one of the Tag Groovi plates to add a greeting embellishment.

How to...

1. Using a pencil, trace the Octagon on to clear parchment paper. This is now the front.
2. Emboss the border design on the reverse using the pencil line as a guide for placement. Erase the pencil line.
3. Emboss the circle and wreath and add the grid design within the circle.
4. Colour the design on the reverse with Perga Colours Exclusive
5. Emboss and colour the tag design.
6.Perforate around the edge and the tag using a 2 needle tool and picot cut.
7. Mount on Rainbow River Designer Paper using Pergamano Brads.

A Birthday Sunrise
Dee Paramour

Ingredients

TINA'S FLORAL DOODLE WREATH
GRO-FL-40830-03
TINA'S FLORAL DOODLE BORDER
GRO-FL-40833-09
NESTED SQUARES EXTENSION & ALPHABET FRAME
GRO-WO-40538-15
NESTED CIRCLES & FRILLY FRAMES
GRO-PA-40554-15
MOUNTAINS & HILLS
GRO-LA-40007-03

Dee has added an amazing landscape to create an entirely different feel to her stunning card.

How to...

1. On pale blue parchment paper, emboss a rectangular frame using the Nested Squares plate and add the floral detail and text.
2. Using the Nestes Circles, create a dome and then create the landscape and scalloped border details. Add colour with Perga Liner pencils on the reverse and cut out.
3. On clear parchment paper, emboss the frame and corner details. Colour with Perga Liner pencils.
4. Attach to white card.

Technicolour Florals
Amanda Williams

Ingredients

TINA'S FLORAL DOODLE WREATH
GRO-FL-40830-03
TINA'S FLORAL DOODLE BORDER
GRO-FL-40833-09
NESTED SQUARES EXTENSION & ALPHABET FRAME
GRO-WO-40538-15

Amanda has used bold colours to create this vivid design.

How to...

1. On ivory parchment paper, emboss the 6th square from the outside of the Nested Squares Extension plate. Perforate with a semi-circle tool and picot cut.
2. Create a frame using the scallop design from the border plate (use a nested square as a guide) on blue parchment and add a row of flowers to create an inner frame.
3. Colour the design with Perga Liner pencils on the front.
5. Perforate the centre of the flowers with the flower perforating tool and picot cut.
6. Using a 2 needle tool, perforate the outer border and picot cut.
7. Layer on to coloured paper and embellish with Boutique paper flowers.

Black Flower Circles

Glynis Whitehead

Ingredients

TINA'S FLORAL DOODLE WREATH
GRO-FL-40830-03
STRAIGHT PATTERN NO. 1 BORDER PIERCING GRID
GRO-GG-40350-14
NESTED SQUARES EXTENSION & ALPHABET FRAME
GRO-WO-40538-15

Glynis has used a faux gem as the focal point on her stylish card.

How to...

1. Trace the floral wreath and inner circle using the Groovi plate with a black fine liner pen (this is the front of the work). Alternatively, you can lightly emboss using a 1.5mm ball tool to create a slight indent and the carefully go over with a black fine line pen whilst still attached to the Groovi Plate.

2. Emboss the 5th & 6th square from the Nested Squares Extension plate.

3. Emboss the grid design.

4. Colour the 'gem' using 3 toning coloured pencils. Add a white highlight with a Pergamano white gel pen.

5. Add whitework to the flowers & leaves.

6. Shallow perforate with a small Picot V tool around the outer border, add an embossed dot within each perforation. Re-perforate & picot cut.

41

Happy Birthday
Maggie Byford

Ingredients

TINA'S FLORAL DOODLE WREATH
GRO-FL-40830-03
NESTED SQUARES EXTENSION & ALPHABET FRAME
GRO-WO-40538-15
TINA'S DOODLE FLOWERS 2
GRO-FL-40757-02
JAYNE'S BUTTERFLIES
GRO-AN-40319-03
LACE 1 BORDER PLATE
GRO-PA-40044-09

Maggie has used Perga Liners pencils to create the soft colour on this beautiful card.

How to...

1. Emboss the 6th square from the outside of the Nested Squares Extension plate and the floral designs within it.
2. Add the lace border and the greetings.
3. Colour on the reverse of the parchment with Perga Liners.
4. Perforate around the border using a 2 needle tool and picot cut.
5. Emboss, colour, perforate and picot cut a butterfly and attach to the centre of the project.
6. Mount on coloured card using Pergamano Brads.

Claritystamp

For You
Jane Telford

Ingredients

TINA'S FLORAL DOODLE WREATH
GRO-FL-40830-03
TINA'S FLORAL DOODLE BORDER
GRO-FL-40833-09
NESTED SQUARES EXTENSION & ALPHABET FRAME
GRO-WO-40538-15
FRAMEWORK CIRCLES
GRO-PA-40722-15
ART DECO ALPHABET GROOVI BORDER PLATE MATE
GRO-MA-40348-13

Jane has combined the Doodle Wreath plates with our Framework Circles plate to create this vibrant card.

How to...

1. Emboss a frame using the 5th & 8th squares from the outside of the Nested Squares plate. Emboss 4 circles within this.
2. Add text using the plate mate and emboss the floral design.
3. Stipple between the circular frames and add whitework to the dots in the design.
4. Colour on the reverse with Perga Colours Exclusive.
5. Perforate around the border using a 2 needle bold tool and picot cut.
6. Add Perga Glitter with Sticky Ink & a Mapping Pen.
7. Attach to coloured card with Pergamano Brads and embellish with sequins.

A Gridwork Wreath
Josie Davidson

Ingredients

TINA'S FLORAL DOODLE WREATH
GRO-FL-40830-03
TINA'S FLORAL DOODLE BORDER
GRO-FL-40833-09
NESTED SQUARES EXTENSION & ALPHABET FRAME
GRO-WO-40538-15
STRAIGHT BASIC A4 GROOVI PIERCING GRID
GRO-GG-40528-17
DIAGONAL BASIC A4 GROOVI PIERCING GRID
GRO-GG-40529-17

Josie has used the floral wreaths to border her lovely grid design.

How to...

1. Create a frame using the 2nd & 3rd squares from the outside of the Nested Square Extension plate. Emboss the floral designs in the centre and each of the corners.
2. Use the 2mm star tool and the Straight Basic A4 grid to create the design within the main circle and each of the corners by combining perforating, embossing and picot cutting.
3. The main background is created using the Diagonal Basic A4 grid to perforate. Add colour on the reverse using Perga Liner pencils.
4. Perforate around the outer border using a 2 needle tool and picot cut.
5. Add Perga Glitter using Sticky Ink and a Mapping Pen.
6. Attach to Rainbow River Designer Paper and add pearls to embellish.

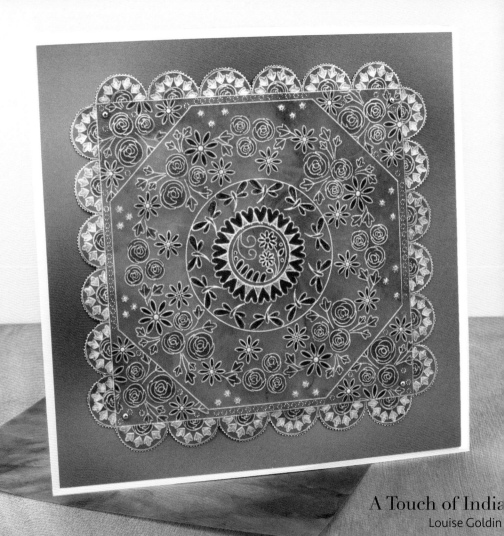

A Touch of India
Louise Goldin

Ingredients

TINA'S ROSIE DOODLE WREATH
GRO-FL-40831-03
TINA'S ROSIE DOODLE BORDER
GRO-FL-40832-09
NESTED SQUARES EXTENSION & ALPHABET FRAME
GRO-WO-40538-15
TINA'S DOODLE FLOWERS 2
GRO-FL-40757-02
OCTAGON EXTENSION & ART DECO ALPHABET
GRO-PA-40552-15

Louise has also used another of Tina's plate designs to create this fabulous card.

How to...

1. Emboss a frame with the smallest octagon shape on Indian Summer Designer Parchment paper. Centre this onto the Nested Squares Extension and emboss a further frame around it.

2. Add the border, floral designs and circle. Emboss the centre design from the Doodle Flowers plate.

3. Add additional using the Pergamano Flower Tool and Pergamano 2mm Star Tool.

4. Colour on the front of the parchment using Perga Liners .

5. Using a 2 needle tool, perforate around the outside edge and picot cut.

6. Attach to Indian Summer Designer Paper using Pergamano Brads.

Flowers for Tina
Jane Telford

Ingredients

TINA'S ROSIE DOODLE WREATH
GRO-FL-40831-03
TINA'S ROSIE DOODLE BORDER
GRO-FL-40832-09
NESTED SQUARES EXTENSION & ALPHABET FRAME
GRO-WO-40538-15
NESTED CIRCLES & FRILLY FRAMES
GRO-PA-40554-15
STRAIGHT PATTERN NO. 1 BORDER PIERCING GRID
GRO-GG-40350-14
STRAIGHT BASIC BORDER PIERCING GRID
GRO-GG-40384-14
TINA'S 3D FLOWERS & BUTTERFLIES
GRO-FL-40553-15

Jane has embellished her design with handmade flowers and leaves.

How to...

1. Emboss the circle with the daisies. Using the nested circles as a guide, emboss the scallop design from the border plate in a circle.

2. Using the nested circles plate, emboss the 5th circle from the centre & add the daisy design inside it.

3. Add a frame using the 5th & 7th from the outside of the Nested Squares Extension plate and emboss the border design.

4. Using the Border Pattern Grid and the Straight Border Grid, emboss, perforate & picot cut the grid details. Personalise with a name.

5. From spare parchment, make two flowers and leaves.

6. Add colour using Perga Colours Exclusive.

7. Attach to a coloured card blank, adding the flower embellishment.